WINNING
WOMEN

QUOTATIONS ON SPORTS, HEALTH & FITNESS

Compiled by
Beth Mende Conny

PETER PAUPER PRESS, INC.
WHITE PLAINS, NEW YORK

To two of my favorite winning women—
my mother, Judy Korotkin,
and my sister, Nina Mende

Copyright © 1993
Peter Pauper Press, Inc.
202 Mamaroneck Avenue
White Plains, NY 10601
All rights reserved
ISBN 0-88088-578-5
Printed in Singapore
7 6 5 4 3 2 1

CONTENTS

INTRODUCTION

Where do you find today's winning women? They're on the courts of Wimbledon, the golf links at Pebble Beach, the basketball courts of Stanford, and the balance beams of Olympic stadiums. You'll find them bike racing through France, surfing in Hawaii, skiing at Lake Placid, and dog sledding in Alaska. Women are fighting bulls in Spain, ice skating in Calgary, swimming rivers in New York, and running marathons in Korea. They're in meets and heats, in the news and on cereal boxes, setting world records and setting new standards for what female athletes can do and have yet to do.

More important, you'll find them wherever you live and work, for, in essence, winning women are those who accept the challenge of being all that they can be. They are the ones who want to experience the joy, pride, and feelings of physical and psychological strength that result from being fabulously fit.

This collection looks at winning women from several perspectives. It offers a unique and intimate view of some of the world's best and most revered female athletes. Through their words, we come to understand the agony and ecstasy of winning, losing, and playing the game. We also come to a greater understanding of their individual sports and the pressures they face as women in a male-dominated field.

Winning Women also examines the how's and why's of getting into—and staying in—shape. It draws on the thoughts, suggestions, and insights of women in the know—fitness experts, actresses, models, and others who appreciate the importance of healthy bodies and positive self-image.

In addition, the collection offers words of inspiration to women determined to do—and be—their personal best, whether that means swimming a faster lap, running an extra mile, accepting and working within their physical limitations, or facing life's myriad challenges.

Finally, *Winning Women* celebrates today's female athlete. It is she who is reshaping the world of sports and redefining women's role within it. It is she who is embracing good health, fitness and self-esteem and opening the door to seemingly endless possibilities. We salute and champion her indomitable spirit and drive.

B. M. C.

WOMEN IN SPORTS

Tennis

I have often been asked whether I am a woman or an athlete. The question is absurd. Men are not asked that. I am an athlete. I am a woman.

BILLIE JEAN KING

A rock'n'roller can put up a fair performance. He needn't even be at his best. In tennis, you have to win.

MONICA SELES

I like to laugh, but on the court, it is my work. I try to smile, but it is so difficult. I concentrate on the ball, not on my face.

STEFFI GRAF

I get different experts sending letters, both sides saying grunting is great for the game, grunting is bad for your game. I don't think anybody knows the real truth.

MONICA SELES

I know what it takes to get through the Open, although I don't think I've mastered it to perfection—you have to block everything out, be extremely focused, and be relaxed and mellow, too.

JENNIFER CAPRIATI

As a top player, you don't want to change, become a little softer or more normal on the outside, because deep down inside, you know that might change your game.

TRACY AUSTIN

As you get older, your life gets a little more complicated. It's a little harder to totally focus on things.

PAM SHRIVER

Billie Jean King taught me a long time ago that tennis players are entertainers. We're all entertainers. That's why we're paid such ridiculous money.

MARTINA NAVRATILOVA

Time is running out. I don't know how much more I have in this head, this heart, these legs.

MARTINA NAVRATILOVA

Everybody cries, if not on the court then in the shower.

YULIA BERBERIAN,
mother of the 3 Maleevas

Sometimes I go out there and I worry about playing the person. But I am at the age where I have to start putting things together.

PATRICIA HY

Bowling

What I love most about bowling, besides the money I earn, is that it is open to anyone. I can bowl against the best or the worst, and it's the same pleasure.

PAULA SPERBER

I'm not a quitter. Bowling is such an emotional sport, things can change quickly. Tomorrow's another day.

LEILA WAGNER

Bull Fighting

Every problem in your life goes away in front of a bull. Because *this* problem, the bull, is bigger than all other problems. Of course I have fear, but it is fear that I will fail the responsibility I have taken on in front of all those people—not fear of the bull. Death becomes unimportant when I am in front of him. I feel so good, it does not matter if he kills me.

CRISTINA SANCHEZ

Cycling

To accept the challenge of the road is to take a journey inside yourself.

CONNIE CARPENTER

Once you get yourself physically conditioned to endure the cycling, time just vanishes. You reach a level where your concentration is extremely deep. I'm not a religious person, but it was God-given to me to use everything I have. For me it's riding a bike.

NANCY RAPOSO

Horseracing/Jumping

What it comes down to is that anybody can win with the best horse. What makes you good is if you can take the second- or third-best horse and win.

VICKY ARAGON

Jumping is a much more technical skill than riding. You've got to be aware of everything at just the right moment.

JULIE KRONE

Golf

I put on my game face because that's
what I need to do to win.

BETSY KING

Golf is such a streaky, mental game. You
take it when you get it, and right now
I'm gettin' it.

BETH DANIEL

If it wasn't for golf, I'd probably be the
fat lady in the circus now.

KATHY WHITWORTH

The pressure I put on myself was so
bad. I had to overcome this question in
my mind, "Can I win again?"

NANCY LOPEZ

I never blame my equipment, but I kept
missing three- and four-foot putts. So I
told myself, Hey, you have got to make
a change. I didn't get rid of my old
putter. I just put it on probation.

Juli Inkster

You start playing for money instead of
trophies and golf becomes a job.

Danielle Ammaccapane

Golf has been a lot like basketball. It's
taken me a long time to make the
starting lineup.

Dawn Coe

Skating

When it comes to a major figure skating
event, the men usually have about as
much chance of upstaging their female
contemporaries as Lawrence Welk
would at a Paula Abdul concert.

Dave Nightingale

It doesn't matter what anybody thinks of what I do. The clock doesn't lie.

BONNIE BLAIR

You need it all: the lightness and the airiness; the music, the personality. You need the caressing of the ice.

CAROL HEISS

I think I look good out there. I'm strong, powerful and artistic. But I have my doubts as much as anyone. And there are so many more things to life than skating—I hope.

JILL TRENARY

Skiing

When you're in the air, you just have to accept that you're in the air and have a good time up there.

KRISTA SCHMIDINGER,
on downhill bumps

I am not afraid of crashing. I never hurt myself because I am a *Glückspilz* [lucky mushroom].

MARIA WALLISER

I can't be worrying about the whole world. When it's time to ski, I've got to be there for me first.

DONNA WEINBRECHT

Swimming

Most people . . . do not understand just how much training takes out of you. It's lonely in that pool. Just think of the countless hours in the water when you scarcely talk to another human being. All you have is that black line. It becomes your best friend.

CATHY FERGUSON

People expect more of twins.

PENNY VILAGOS,
synchronized swimmer
with twin, Vicky

I do best in events that take a long time
to train for and to complete. I may not
be the fastest athlete around, but I also
get a kick out of logistically complicated
events. I'm like the general who loves
strategizing and managing complicated
logistics.

MAG DONALDSON

I am willing to put myself through
anything; temporary pain or discomfort
means nothing to me as long as I can
see that the experience will take me to a
new level. I am interested in the
unknown, and the only path to the
unknown is through breaking barriers,
an often-painful process.

DIANA NYAD

Surfing

[Life] is a surf movie. You're either in it
or you're watching it.

PENNY KEATING

Sometimes the water goes so fast
beneath you it seems it will tear your
wetsuit right off. You can feel the whole
ocean rushing along your belly. Nothing
matters—work, outside pressures—
everything goes away, and all that's left
is a sense of peace.

LAUREN CRUX

The ocean is not a threat, it's an
opportunity to be in harmony with
nature, with godliness.

LAUREN CRUX

Surfing is so different from other sports.
It's not like competing on a track, a
tennis court, or a ski slope. Every day
something changes—the waves, the
ocean bottom, the swell directions, the
tide. It never gets old, never. What
Nature has provided us with gives a
challenging, conquering feeling—a real
rush when you ride the big waves.

ALISA SCHWARZSTEIN

Archery

Archery isn't like track and field, where you can use your excitement to help you run faster. You have to be steady all the time. You have to work with your movements. Archery uses a flowing motion. If it becomes jerky, that usually means you're not shooting well.

DENISE PARKER

Rowing

There is the aesthetic value, the challenge of trying to match the rhythm of another physical being while trying to achieve flow in the movement of the boat. You're always looking for the perfect row.

VIKKI SCOTT

It's a feeling you get when you're paddling, using all your muscles and gliding. It's fun, almost medicinal. It's rhythmic, it's hypnotic, yet I like how I feel afterward. It's like a runner's high.

CATHY MARINO

Track and Field

Running was very important. It was something that kept me busy and something I really grew to love. I had fun with it. My friends ran too. It was just something we did every day, like brushing our teeth. I took it from there.

SUZY HAMILTON

If you want to become the best runner you can be, start now. That's all I did. Don't spend the rest of your life wondering if you could do it.

PRISCILLA WELCH

No pain, no Spain.

GWEN TORRENCE

The obstacle is the thing. The bar is the
answer to the question of whether you
are successful. It's always there. If you
make it, it goes up. The challenge is
constant, and that's what I want.

LOUISE RITTER

For me it's the challenge—the challenge
to try to beat myself or do better than I
did in the past. I try to keep in mind not
what I have accomplished but what I
have to try to accomplish in the future.

JACKIE JOYNER-KERSEE

I enjoy running because it's very black
and white. There's no making up stories.
It's not a popularity contest or a
subjective thing. Run good or run bad,
you're the one that did it.

JANE WELZEL

When I run, I think of the parts of my life that made me what I am: my grandmother, my childhood friends, my community. Running makes me feel loved. It makes me want to go on and on.

Essie Garrett

Dogsled Racing

I don't go to movies or watch TV. I don't live near any towns. I don't do anything that takes my time. Everything is put into the dogs. The fact that I put so much time in with my dogs from the time they're born makes for a dog that's *that* much better.

Susan Butcher,
Iditarod champion

THE FEMALE ATHLETE

I look at the '70s as a time when the American public accepted women athletes; the '80s as a time it supported them; and the '90s will be a time for America to embrace women in sport.

MERRILY DEAN BAKER

The new female consciousness that has developed over the last decade extends to our right to physical as well as economic, political and social equality. We not only need to develop and extend our physical limits, we want to. And we refuse to be afraid that we will no longer be considered attractive and acceptable when we are strong. We now recognize the strong, healthy woman who has fulfilled her physical potential, as beautiful.

JANE FONDA

Let's face it: Bo might know baseball, but he doesn't know a thing about visible panty lines. If sporting goods companies want our dollars, they've got to start speaking our language.

SUSANNA LEVIN

If I were a man, I would run. Most men matadors do. But if I run, someone in the audience will yell that I am running because I am a woman and I am scared—so I will not run.

CRISTINA SANCHEZ

Martina Navratilova is not a "girl," nor is Debi Thomas or Katarina Witt, and the women skaters weren't "cute" in 1988. The problem with describing women as girls is that they never grow up and therefore can't take positions of authority in the world of sport. But the good news is that you can change language, so ultimately you can change the picture of women in sports.

ANITA DE FRANTZ

I think about coming here to go as high
as I can. I come here to try to stop 100-
mile-per-hour pucks. I have a lot of
pressure on me, so I don't think about
anything except stopping pucks.

MANON RHEAUME

Freedom to explore our environment
and develop our bodily abilities is a link
to intellectual development.

GLORIA STEINEM

I always tell my girls: think like a man,
but act and look like a woman.

CAROL HEISS

From the seat of a bicycle, there is little
difference in how a man or woman
experiences the world. But there is a
great disparity between the way the
world treats a man by himself and the
way it treats a woman cycling alone.

WILLAMARIE HUELSKAMP

A smart woman can be competitive against a stronger man simply by using common sense and intuition. But being competitive doesn't necessarily mean wanting to win races.

Connie Carpenter Phinney

Male coaches hold women back. Their egos are threatened.

Bob Kersee

I think girls are much more competitive than boys. Some track coaches may say the opposite, but that's because they've never coached women.

Fred Thompson

The men are like rock'n'roll stars. We don't live in that fast lane, with the celebrity status. If we can sneak into that shadow, we'll get more attention, and that's not bad.

Nancy Lieberman-Cline

If a task of any kind is perceived as somehow sex-specific, then society will discourage people of the opposite sex from participating. This has been the case with women and sports.

CHUCK CORBIN

Women are carrying a new attitude. They've cast aside the old stereotypes. They don't believe you have to be ugly or have big muscles to play sports.

SHIRBEY JOHNSON

Being a woman in this business is like being left-handed. People tell you all your life you have to do it with your right hand, and you try and it just isn't right. We get the same results [as male sportswriters] but we're a little different. We have this great southpaw delivery.

SALLY JENKINS,
sportswriter

My 6-year-old daughter plays T-ball and
soccer; if my wife had done that as a
child, she would have been called a
tomboy. There are no more tomboys.

GREG RORKE

The overemphasis on protecting girls
from strain or injury and underemphasis
on developing skills and experiencing
teamwork fits neatly into the pattern of
the second sex. . . . Girls are the
spectators and the cheerleaders. . . .
Perfect preparation for the adult role of
woman—to stand decoratively on the
sidelines of history and cheer on the
men who make the decisions.

KATHRYN CLARENBACH

Boys who were athletic got scholarships;
girls who were good at sports had their
sexuality questioned.

JANET SACHS

The sooner little boys begin to realize
that little girls are equal and that there
will be many opportunities for a boy to
be bested by a girl, the closer they will
be to better mental health.

SYLVIA PRESSLER

As women win more and more gains in
the drive for equality and as the
traditional roles begin to blur and fuse,
the exclusivity of men's sports seems to
become even more entrenched. In fact,
in many ways sports seem to be a kind
of last bastion of male supremacy.

KATHRYN LANCE

There is no life for girls in team sports
past Little League.

BILLIE JEAN KING

"Athlete" is a fine, strong word. And like
the simple act of softening a new leather
mitt with an eager fist, there's nothing
female or male about it.

MARIAH BURTON NELSON

WINNING AND LOSING

Personal sacrifices are really the beginning and the end of everything, because you don't win because you do one thing right or two things right. You win because you do 1,000 little things right throughout the year.

SUSAN BUTCHER

If you can react the same way to winning and losing, that . . . quality is important because it stays with you the rest of your life.

CHRIS EVERT

Neither Huang nor I places much importance in winning the gold. We believe victory in competition is the reward for difficult training, much like a farmer reaps a good harvest after a year's hard work in the field.

KAN FULIN

Sport is sport, and the strongest win.

SVETLANA BOGINSKAYA

Money was never a goal for me because of my amateur training. I was taught to win, and that was it.

JOANNE CARNER

The main thing is not a matter of wanting to win; the main thing is being scared to lose.

BILLIE JEAN KING

I always thought that the person who works the hardest, apart from natural talent, of course, wins. I feel the person who works the hardest *earns* the right to win.

KATY BILODEAUX

It's hard to stay patient when you want to win so badly.

CAREN KEMNER

The major joy of most sports is the process, the playing of the sport and the physical release that it brings. But winning, or at least being as good as you can be, is a major part of sports, and you can experience that aspect only by developing your own toughness, physical and mental.

KATHRYN LANCE

You're *nothing* if you don't win. This is all you have in the world, nothing else.

JULIE KRONE

You can't be scared to win. When you win, you *let* yourself win.

AMY ALCOTT

You've got to win in sports—that's talent—but you've also got to learn how to remind everybody how you did win, and how often. That comes with experience.

BILLIE JEAN KING

When you've got kids to worry about, a double bogey isn't the end of the world.

MYRA BLACKWELDER

I still hate to lose, but now that I've seen a little more of the world, I know it's not the end of the world. I watch TV and see there's so many wrong things, dying children, so how can you cry about a stupid match?

JENNIFER CAPRIATI

I'm all for enjoyment, but it is a little tough when your opponent is just laughing after she aces you.

MARTINA NAVRATILOVA

Now when I lose a match, I know I lose on the court—not in life.

GABRIELA SABATINI

COMPETITION

Before, I was always fighting the bit about competing against someone. I was tired of competing, but I wanted to use my ability. I just didn't want to skate to beat someone else. I wanted to skate for the love of it.

JANET LYNN

There's no one that I hate to play against. I consider everyone a challenge.

STEFFI GRAF

I've never feared any one person. If you fear people, you're going to play into their race plans and what they're thinking.

MARY DECKER SLANEY

I don't have to be enemies with someone to be competitors with them.

JACKIE JOYNER-KERSEE

I focus in my heart and my inner strength is very important to me. I try to establish an inner oneness with the other runners and I compete against myself.

SUPRABHA BECKJORD

I'm very aggressive on the track. But I'm friends with a lot of my competitors, and if I'm not friends with them, it just means I don't know them yet.

SUZY HAMILTON

I don't care whether the person in the next lane is the world-record holder or Helen Keller. I run my own race.

JUDI BROWN-KING

Competition can damage self-esteem, create anxiety and lead to cheating and hurt feelings. But so can romantic love.

MARIAH BURTON NELSON

I want opponents to say, "Hit her. Stop her. Oh, no, here she comes again."

SAM JONES

I'm not going to waste an effort. When I race, it's for business.

SHELLY STEELY

I don't say good luck to people. In my mind I get real cutthroat. If I was swimming against my best friend, I'd start saying bad words against her. I make my competitor my enemy.

KRISZTINA EGERSZEGI

We always think of competition as being about winning, but it really has to do with setting and accomplishing personal goals. Even if that goal is to just cross a finish line.

SUZANNE STRICKLIN MACDONALD

WORDS OF INSPIRATION

As simple as it sounds, we all must try
to be the best person we can: by making
the best choices, by making the most of
the talents we've been given, by treating
others as we would like to be treated.

MARY LOU RETTON

Everything depends on your mental
outlook toward life. If you have a
defeatist attitude, it's bad. It's the same
with a golf game. It's something you
have to work on all the time.

KATHY WHITWORTH

I don't need my happiness, my well-
being, to be based on winning or losing.
That part of my life is over. My life is
more vague now. But it's also more
adventurous and mysterious. Each day
brings some little piece of happiness I
never allowed myself to experience
when I was playing.

CHRIS EVERT

Ninety-eight percent of success is in the head and the heart.

CATHY FERGUSON

I never look back. I want to look at what comes next. Dwelling too much on what's already happened—good or bad—will drain you.

MARY DECKER SLANEY

I spent the '70s trying to fix the world and the '80s trying to fix boyfriends. I'm going to spend the '90s fixing myself. I want to be able to run the Boston Marathon when I'm 70.

ROBERTA GIBB

If we rebuild our physical selves, there is a lot we can do. . . . Strong and painless, we will be able to change our world for the better.

BONNIE PRUDDEN

I tried not to let anyone direct my life if they weren't me.

LOUISE RITTER

Unless you strike out 21 of 21 and hit a homerun—no, a grand slam—there's *always* something better you can do. Always.

MICHELE GRANGER

Your goals always reflect your resources.

DONNA LOPIANO

When anyone tells me I can't do anything, why, I'm just not listening any more.

FLORENCE GRIFFITH JOYNER

EXERCISE

I've got to do something about getting in shape. But things keep getting in the way. Things like my shape, to begin with.

MARY Z. GRAY

There are dozens of ways to get into shape, to improve the way you look and how you feel. But before anything can change, you have to make a commitment to yourself. And most of all you have to want the end results.

LINDA EVANS

My number-one exercise for all women is to use their ears. Listen to your own words about yourself and the way your body looks.

KAYLAN PICKFORD

As far as beauty is concerned, in order to be confident we must accept that the way we look and feel is our own responsibility.

SOPHIA LOREN

I don't work out. If God wanted us to bend over, he'd put diamonds on the floor.

JOAN RIVERS

Many busy people are overwhelmed by the idea of fitness, so they do nothing. Part of the problem lies with our fitness role models. People like Jane Fonda and Arnold Schwarzenegger work out for several hours every day—but that's beyond fitness. That's appearance.

MARY ANNE BENTON

Today's self-improvement tack is, of course, physical. Like medieval flagellants, we are supposed to whip our muscles into line and beat our cellulite into shape. It is no longer enough to walk in the path of righteousness, we have to run in it.

ELLEN GOODMAN

Writing a large check to a health spa doesn't count as exercise.

LINDA STASI

Fitness begins with a conscious decision
to make it a top priority in your life.
Remember: You can take off those
shoes, but taking off those thighs takes a
lot more doing.

VICTORIA PRINCIPAL

I've noticed it's harder to stay in shape. I
have to work twice as hard for half the
results.

CHRISTIE BRINKLEY

Physical fitness programs are something
I personally avoid, like trips to the
dentist. The way I look at it, a woman
gets a complete workout every time she
goes to the supermarket.

MARY KUCZKIR

Exercise is a selfish venture in the most
positive sense.

DOROTHY HARRIS

First of all, let's get one thing straight: fitness and exercise aren't the same thing. You can exercise without getting fit, but you can't get fit without exercise.

JACLYN SMITH

Sure, you can tone up your thighs, but if you don't understand that your thigh is part of your leg, and your leg is part of a physical and mental system, and *that* system is part of a whole social system, then you're missing out on an awful lot.

KATHY SMITH

Sure, having an attractive figure is a wonderful reason to get into a regular, enjoyable pattern of exercise. But America's fitness boom has spawned a new breed I call fitness bores.

JACLYN SMITH

Your body tells you in its way when you feel good emotionally.

STEFFI GRAF

Let fitness be your launching point.
Picture exercise as the hub of a wheel
with spokes that jut into every area of
your life.

JUDI SHEPPARD MISSETT

From long observation, and brief
participation, I can tell you that running
is dreadful. The psychic rewards don't
come from oxygen; they come from
overcoming the desire to quit, squelching
the urge to stop this infernal nonsense
and lie down.

ELLEN GOODMAN

Scientists change their minds every
twenty minutes about what drugs are
good for you, and what kind of
counseling best helps your psyche, and
even what *kinds* of exercise are the most
fruitful—but there's one thing they
never change their minds about, and
that is the fact that some kind of exercise
is essential to everyone.

CRISTINA FERRARE

It takes intense concentration and precision, a combination of physical and psychic energy. When I leave [the gym after boxing] I am clear, self-confident and peaceful.

WENDY G. FINCH

To me, exercising without physical awareness seems a little like making love while wearing ski clothes: sure, you can probably maneuver it, but you're certainly going to miss out on the subtleties, if not the purpose of the whole experience.

KATHY SMITH

Exercise is powerful preventive medicine.

JUDI SHEPPARD MISSETT

Exercise makes you more graceful. When you exercise you walk as if you own the street—with pride and fluidity.

SOPHIA LOREN

BODY IMAGE

We wear our attitudes in our bodies, and
I grew up looking like a question mark:
Am I okay? Do you approve?

PATTI DAVIS

The only practical, permanent solution
to poor body image seems to be turning
inward to ask: *Where did it come from?*

GLORIA STEINEM

The majority of women in our culture
do not accept their bodies as they are. In
fact, it is a rare woman today who has a
healthy body image, who is not actively
doing battle with her body.

MARCIA GERMAINE

To me, good health is more than just
exercise and diet. It's really a point of
view and a mental attitude you have
about yourself.

ANGELA LANSBURY

Your body plays an integral part in your life. It is not just the family car for trips around town. It is also the golden "all-terrain vehicle" in which you live and create adventures.

SUZY PRUDDEN

Health of body is not only an accompaniment of health of mind, but is the cause; the converse may be true— that health of mind causes health of body; but we all know that intellectual cheer and vivacity act upon the mind. If the gymnastic exercise helps the mind, the concert or the theatre improves the health of the body.

MARIA MITCHELL

As long as my body is in shape, my mind works at its full capacity.

VICTORIA PRINCIPAL

MRS. MOLLISON

Sedentary people are apt to have sluggish minds. A sluggish mind is apt to be reflected in flabbiness of body and in a dullness of expression that invites no interest and gets none.

ROSE FITZGERALD KENNEDY

To regain a healthy sense of self-worth I first had to break down old fears and doubts and anxieties. Only then was I able to reshape my image successfully. Now, my exterior and interior are in harmony. I really feel as good as I look. And dammit, I know I look good.

ELIZABETH TAYLOR

Your thoughts about yourself are not arbitrary—you create them. Whether they are positive or negative, you can use them as keys to unlock a greater sensitivity to what your body needs to be its healthy, beautiful best.

KAYLAN PICKFORD

A WOMAN'S BODY

Your body is your center. It is the only one you have—and it is the vehicle that will take you through life.

JUDI SHEPPARD MISSETT

It seems to be forgotten that everyday life can become a playground of sensual awareness when the body is fit and well tuned.

DIANA NYAD

We must begin at the beginning, just as the gardener who wants beautiful flowers in summer must start by cultivating the soil and properly nourishing the seedlings that come up in the early spring. The human organism needs an ample supply of good building material to repair the effects of daily wear and tear.

INDRA DEVI

Being in good shape is not just looking good. A good physical condition is protection. Our strength comes from our body. The fact that I was hit by a car and not torn to pieces or killed is proof of that. My muscles were so toned and so strong they literally saved my life!

JANICE DARLING

The mind and the heart sometimes get another chance, but if anything happens to the poor old human frame, why, it's just out of luck, that's all.

KATHERINE ANNE PORTER

The ancient Greeks believed in the ideal of "a sound mind in a sound body." For myself, at least, and I believe for most women, the one cannot exist without the other, and the two reinforce each other in every way.

KATHRYN LANCE

When you think of the bodily soundness which is necessary to success in life, to effectiveness in your adult life, think of the wiry, tough, active, enduring body which resists fatigue, and endures anxiety without a quiver, and faces danger in the same way.

GEORGE SAND

I am sure that one's innate intelligence and instinct for good can be enhanced through fitness.

JANE FONDA

Society feels that sport must be justified, and we have gotten away from the Greek concept of mind and body. That is a failure of the physical education process.

OLGA CONNOLLY

PLAYING THE GAME

The playing of a game has to do with
your feelings, your emotions, how you
care about the people you're involved
with.

VIVIAN STRINGER

I've swum for my country, I've swum for
my coaches and my schools and my
teams. I decided this time I was going to
swim for me.

JANET EVANS

An athlete rarely has a chance to take
him or herself to the limit, and then go
on. I know if I ever have to, I can do it. I
can take it to the very end. Not many
people can say that. And it's a feeling I
can hang on to forever.

JULIE MOSS

When I was 15, I had lucky underwear.
When that failed, I had a lucky hairdo,
then a lucky race number, even lucky
race days. After 15 years, I've found the
secret to success is simple. It's hard
work.

MARGARET GROOS

I always thought of my career as a
marathon. You want to quit every step of
the way, but something inside keeps you
from doing it.

KATHY JOHNSON

In the field of sports you are more-or-
less accepted for what you do rather
than what you are.

ALTHEA GIBSON DARBON

The public doesn't know the stress you are under. All of a sudden you get all this stuff thrown at you—the fame, the money. You're thrown into this public image, into upholding "the dreams of the American people," and the press is there with all these expectations, and you're 19 or 20 and all you want to do is go to the prom.

ROSALYNN SUMNERS

I have never thought of participating in sports just for the sake of doing it for exercise or as a means to lose weight. And I've never taken up a sport just because it was a social fad. I really enjoy playing. It is a vital part of my life.

DINAH SHORE

The climb back is harder than the climb up for any athlete.

DEB RICHARD

This is the worst time of all, the couple
of seconds before the music starts. It
may seem not much more than the blink
of an eye but time seems to stand still as
you wait and wonder if something
might go wrong.

JANE TORVILL

I can't say I like having pressure on me.
I don't think anybody does. But
somehow it brings out the best in me.
There's always that nervous feeling, that
twinge in your stomach, and I don't
know if it means I'm anxious or just
ready to go. But I think it's something
that every competitor has, and I need
that.

MARY LOU RETTON

Marathon swimming is the most difficult
physical, intellectual and emotional
battleground I have encountered, and
each time I win, each time I touch the
other shore, I feel worthy of any other
challenge life has to offer.

DIANA NYAD